Workbook

for

The Gift of Fear

Survival Signals That Protect Us from Violence

A Practical Guide to Gavin de Becker's Book

Gelena Reads

This workbook is intended solely for educational and personal use. It is designed to complement and enhance the original book, **The Gift of Fear**, written **by Gavin de Becker.** The workbook provides exercises, activities, and additional content to aid in understanding and applying the concepts presented in the original book.

Please note that this workbook is not a substitute for the original book. It is recommended that readers use this workbook in conjunction with the original book to maximize their learning experience and comprehension of the subject matter.

How To Use This Workbook

Welcome to the companion workbook for "**The Gift of Fear: Survival Signals That Protect Us from Violence" by Gavin de Becker.** This workbook is designed to be used alongside the original book to enhance your understanding of the key concepts and to help you apply them to your own life. By engaging with the content in this workbook, you will gain valuable insights into recognizing and responding to potential threats, building your intuition, and fostering personal safety and well-being.

Chapter by Chapter Summary:
This workbook begins with a comprehensive chapter-by-chapter summary of the main points covered in the original book. This summary serves as a quick refresher of the key insights and prepares you for the in-depth exploration that follows.

Key Lessons:
Each chapter in this workbook delves into the core lessons presented in the corresponding chapter of "The Gift of Fear." These key lessons highlight the fundamental takeaways that will empower you to identify danger signals, trust your instincts, and navigate potentially threatening situations.

Self-Reflection Questions:

Throughout the workbook, you will encounter thought-provoking self-reflection questions related to the material covered. These questions are designed to encourage introspection and deepen your understanding of the concepts. Take your time to ponder these questions and write down your responses in the spaces provided. Your insights will serve as valuable reference points for your personal growth journey.

Life-Changing Exercises:
To make the principles of "The Gift of Fear" applicable to your everyday life, this workbook offers a series of life-changing exercises. These exercises are hands-on activities that allow you to put theory into practice. By engaging with these exercises, you will develop practical skills that can help you respond effectively to potential threats and challenging situations.

Self-Assessment Questions:
At the end of this workbook, you will find a section dedicated to self-assessment questions. These questions will help you gauge your progress and understanding of the concepts covered in both the original book and this workbook. Be honest with yourself as you answer these questions, as they are intended to support your personal development and ensure that you are gaining valuable insights from this learning experience.

How to Maximize Your Learning:
To make the most of this workbook, we recommend the following steps:

1. Start by reading the chapter-by-chapter summary to refresh your memory of the main book's content.
2. Progress through each chapter, paying close attention to the key lessons, self-reflection questions, and life-changing exercises.
3. Take your time to thoughtfully answer the self-reflection questions, as these insights are vital for your personal growth.
4. Engage fully in the life-changing exercises to develop practical skills based on the book's teachings.
5. At the end of the workbook, assess your progress by answering the self-assessment questions honestly.
6. Remember that personal growth is an ongoing process, and revisiting this workbook and the original book periodically can reinforce your knowledge and skills.

Congratulations on taking this step toward empowering yourself with the knowledge and tools to enhance your safety and well-being. Let's embark on this journey together as we explore the profound wisdom of "The Gift of Fear" and apply it to your life in transformative ways. Stay committed to learning and growing, and trust your instincts as you navigate the path towards a safer and more confident you.

Chapter by Chapter Summary

Chapter 1: In the Presence of Danger

In this opening chapter, "The Gift of Fear" introduces you to the concept of intuition and its crucial role in detecting danger. Gavin de Becker emphasizes the importance of trusting your instincts and intuition when it comes to your personal safety. He discusses real-life situations and examples where individuals ignored their gut feelings, leading to tragic outcomes. By sharing stories of people who successfully used their intuition to escape dangerous situations, de Becker sets the stage for understanding the powerful survival signals that our intuition sends us.

Chapter 2: The Technology of Intuition

Building upon the foundation laid in the first chapter, this section explores the mechanism of intuition as a survival tool. Gavin de Becker delves into the scientific and psychological aspects of our intuition, explaining how it draws on past experiences and subtle cues in our environment to make rapid judgments about potential threats. Understanding how our intuition operates as a highly evolved and efficient system for detecting danger enables you to harness its power to protect yourself effectively.

Chapter 3: The Academy of Prediction

In this chapter, de Becker delves deeper into the subject of prediction and how we can learn to recognize and respond to potential danger. He discusses the Academy of Prediction as a metaphor for developing our instincts and honing our ability to foresee danger. By examining pre-incident indicators and patterns of behavior, you'll gain valuable insights into how to identify potential threats and stay vigilant in various situations.

Chapter 4: Survival Signals

Moving on, "The Gift of Fear" introduces you to the concept of survival signals, which are the intuitive cues that warn you of imminent danger. Gavin de Becker explains the various types of survival signals, such as fear, anxiety, and discomfort, and how they serve as invaluable tools for your safety. Recognizing these signals and learning to interpret them accurately can empower you to take proactive steps to protect yourself from harm.

Chapter 5: Imperfect Strangers

This chapter delves into the theme of strangers and the risks associated with encounters involving people we don't know well. Gavin de Becker outlines the potential dangers posed by individuals who seem charming or harmless on the surface but may conceal malevolent intentions. He provides practical advice on how to assess the true nature of strangers and ways to respond to situations where you feel uncomfortable or threatened.

Chapter 6: High-Stakes Predictions

Here, the focus is on situations that involve high stakes, such as life-threatening encounters and violent confrontations. Gavin de Becker discusses the critical importance of listening to your intuition in such scenarios, where rapid decision-making can be a matter of life or death. He shares stories of individuals who accurately predicted danger and took decisive action to survive, illustrating the life-saving potential of trusting your intuition when facing extreme risks.

Chapter 7: Promises to Kill (Understanding Threats)

In this chapter, de Becker delves into the subject of threats and how to assess their seriousness. He explains the different types of threats and the motivations behind them. By understanding the psychology of individuals who make threats, you'll gain valuable insights into their intentions and the level of risk they pose. The chapter also covers ways to respond to threats effectively and the importance of involving law enforcement when necessary.

Chapter 8: Persistence, Persistence (Dealing with people who refuse to let go)

In this chapter, you delve into the challenging issue of dealing with individuals who refuse to let go and persistently pursue their targets. Gavin de Becker emphasizes that when someone continues to pursue you despite your clear disinterest or rejection, it is essential to trust your instincts and take their behavior seriously. He explains that persistence is often a warning sign, and dismissing it as harmless can lead to dangerous situations.

De Becker provides numerous examples of persistent individuals and shares insights on how to respond effectively. He highlights the importance of setting clear boundaries and maintaining consistent responses to discourage unwanted attention. He discusses the concept of "fear without solutions" and how people who are persistent in their pursuit often exploit this fear to manipulate their targets.

Through real-life case studies, you learn about various types of persistent individuals, including stalkers, former intimate partners, and strangers fixated on their targets. De Becker provides practical advice on recognizing warning signs, documenting incidents, and seeking appropriate legal and law enforcement assistance when necessary. He emphasizes the significance of trusting your intuition and seeking help from professionals who specialize in dealing with persistent individuals.

Chapter 9: Occupational Hazards (Violence in the workplace)

In this chapter, you explore the issue of violence in the workplace and the warning signs that precede such incidents. De Becker stresses that workplace violence is a significant concern, and ignoring red flags can have devastating consequences. He discusses the different forms workplace violence can take, ranging from threats and intimidation to physical harm and even fatal attacks.

De Becker provides valuable insights into the pre-incident indicators that can help identify potentially violent individuals in the workplace. He emphasizes the importance of recognizing behaviors such as obsession with weapons, erratic or aggressive behavior, and patterns of blaming others. By paying attention to these warning signs, you can take proactive measures to protect yourself and others.

The chapter also addresses the crucial role of employers and organizations in creating a safe work environment. De Becker discusses the responsibility of employers to establish policies and procedures that address threats and ensure the well-being of their employees. He provides guidance on developing threat assessment teams and implementing effective security measures to mitigate the risk of workplace violence.

Chapter 10: Intimate Enemies (Domestic violence)

In this chapter, you delve into the complex issue of domestic violence, focusing on the dynamics and warning signs of abusive relationships. De Becker highlights that domestic violence is not limited to physical abuse but encompasses various forms of control and manipulation, including emotional, psychological, and financial abuse.

Drawing from his extensive experience in threat assessment, de Becker provides invaluable insights into the patterns and characteristics of abusive relationships. He emphasizes that domestic violence is not a spontaneous act but a predictable pattern of behavior. By understanding the warning signs and red flags, you can identify potential abusers and take steps to protect yourself or someone you care about.

De Becker discusses the importance of recognizing the cycle of violence, power and control dynamics, and the tactics abusers use to maintain dominance over their victims. He emphasizes the significance of developing a safety plan and seeking professional help when dealing with domestic violence situations.

Chapter 11: "I Was Trying to Let Him Down Easy" (Date-stalking)

In this chapter, you explore the issue of date-stalking and the potential dangers that can arise from unwanted attention in dating situations. De Becker emphasizes the importance of recognizing and responding to warning signs during the early stages of a relationship to prevent dangerous outcomes.

Through real-life examples, de Becker illustrates the various tactics employed by date-stalkers and the impact on their targets' lives. He emphasizes that dismissing red flags or feeling obligated to be polite can escalate the risks associated with persistent and obsessive behavior.

De Becker provides practical advice on how to respond effectively to unwanted attention while prioritizing your safety. He emphasizes the significance of trust-building behaviors and clear communication in establishing healthy relationships. Additionally, he provides guidance on developing exit strategies and seeking support from friends, family, and professionals when needed.

Chapter 12: Fear of Children (Violent children)

In this chapter, you explore a challenging topic: violence perpetrated by children. De Becker acknowledges that it can be uncomfortable to discuss violence involving minors, but he emphasizes the importance of recognizing and addressing the issue to protect both potential victims and the children themselves.

De Becker presents case studies and examines the factors that contribute to violent behavior in children. He discusses the role of neglect, exposure to violence, and a lack of appropriate intervention and support systems in shaping their actions. He emphasizes the need for early identification and intervention to prevent further harm.

The chapter also delves into the topic of bullying and its connection to future violent behavior. De Becker provides strategies for parents, educators, and communities to create safer environments for children. He stresses the importance of fostering empathy, establishing clear boundaries, and addressing the underlying issues that lead to violent behavior.

Chapter 13: Better to Be Wanted by the Police Than Not to Be Wanted at All (Attacks against public figures)

In this chapter, you explore the unique challenges and risks faced by public figures, including celebrities, politicians, and high-profile individuals. De Becker sheds light on the heightened threat environment surrounding public figures and the motivations behind attacks against them.

Drawing from his experiences working with prominent clients, de Becker provides insights into the warning signs and indicators that precede attacks on public figures. He discusses the role of fixation, resentment, and ideological beliefs in driving individuals to target those in the public eye.

De Becker emphasizes the importance of security measures, threat assessment, and proactive planning to mitigate risks for public figures. He also addresses the psychological impact of living under constant threat and provides guidance on managing fear and maintaining personal well-being in such circumstances.

Chapter 14: Extreme Hazards

In this chapter, you delve into the realm of extreme hazards and the unique challenges they present. De Becker examines extraordinary situations such as terrorism, hostage-taking, and acts of mass violence. He emphasizes that although these events are rare, it is crucial to be prepared and equipped with the knowledge to respond effectively.

De Becker provides insights into the warning signs and indicators that may precede extreme hazards. He discusses situational awareness, the importance of recognizing pre-incident indicators, and the significance of reporting suspicious activities to the authorities.

The chapter also addresses the psychological impact of extreme hazards and provides guidance on developing resilience and coping strategies in the face of such events. De Becker emphasizes the importance of community preparedness, effective communication, and collaboration with law enforcement agencies to enhance overall safety.

Chapter 15: The Gift of Fear

In the final chapter of the book, de Becker reflects on the overarching theme of the "gift of fear" and its transformative power in protecting us from violence. He highlights that fear is a natural and valuable instinct that should not be ignored or dismissed.

De Becker emphasizes the importance of listening to your intuition and trusting your instincts. He encourages readers to embrace their fear as a valuable source of information and motivation for taking proactive measures to ensure personal safety.

The chapter concludes with a message of empowerment, reminding readers that they possess the ability to assess and respond to potential threats. By learning from the experiences shared throughout the book and honing their intuition, individuals can navigate their lives with increased confidence, security, and peace of mind.

Chapter 1: In the Presence of Danger

Key Lessons

1. Intuition as an Internal Guardian: Intuition is a powerful internal guardian that can warn us of potential dangers and guide us through risky situations. Learning to trust and listen to our intuition can be a life-saving skill.

2. Recognizing Survival Signals: People often ignore or downplay early warning signs and survival signals, leading to increased vulnerability. Being aware of and acknowledging these signals can help us make better decisions in dangerous situations.

3. The Subtle Clues of Danger: Dangerous individuals may present themselves in friendly or charming ways, making it important to pay attention to subtle cues that suggest something is off or potentially dangerous.

4. Overcoming Denial: Denial can prevent us from accepting the possibility of danger, leading to a false sense of security. Accepting that violence can happen to anyone and in any environment can better prepare us to avoid potential risks.

5. Fear as an Ally: Fear, when understood and managed properly, can be a valuable ally. It can empower us to take appropriate actions in the face of danger and increase our chances of survival.

6. Predictability of Violence: Understanding the prevalence of violence in society and acknowledging that it can be predicted, to some extent, can motivate us to take proactive steps to protect ourselves and others from potential harm.

Self-reflection Questions

1. Are you paying enough attention to your intuition and survival signals in potentially risky situations?

_____

_____

_____

_____

_____

_____

2. Do you tend to dismiss subtle cues or warning signs when interacting with others, potentially putting yourself at risk?

_____

_____

_____

_____

_____

_____

_____

3. How can you overcome denial and accept that violence can happen anywhere, enabling you to take proactive steps to enhance your safety?

_____

_____

_____

_____

_____

_____

Life-changing Exercises

1. Practice tuning into your intuition daily and act on its signals.

2. Make a list of potential survival signals in different situations and discuss them with a trusted friend or family member.

3. Pay attention to your gut feelings when meeting new people and use those cues to guide your interactions.

4. Challenge yourself to recognize and address denial in your life, particularly regarding the possibility of violence.

5. Create a safety plan for different scenarios, including how to respond to potential threats.

6. Engage in role-playing exercises to practice assertiveness and boundary-setting in challenging situations.

7. Educate yourself on the patterns of violence in your community and learn strategies to reduce your risk.

Chapter 2: The Technology of Intuition

Key Lessons

1. Intuition is a powerful survival signal: Intuition is a cognitive process that operates at lightning speed and is far more efficient than conscious logical thinking. It is nature's way of warning us about potential dangers and threats.

2. Intuition is not supernatural: People often dismiss intuition as a coincidence or gut feeling, but it is a natural and inherent ability that we all possess. It works by evaluating various factors in our environment and providing us with quick insights without conscious awareness.

3. Intuition and expertise: Even experts rely on intuition, but they may sometimes disregard it due to their over-reliance on known patterns and familiarity with certain situations. Beginners, on the other hand, may embrace intuition more readily because they are open to all possibilities.

4. Trusting intuition over judgment: Our judgment can sometimes cloud our perception and intuition. It's crucial to listen to our inner voice and honor our

feelings, especially when they signal potential danger or unease.

5. Paying attention to extra details: Intuition often works by picking up on seemingly unimportant details in our surroundings. These extra details, called "satellites," can provide valuable information that we may not consciously recognize.

6. Overcoming societal biases: In society, we may prioritize certain risks over others and ignore the intuitive signals about personal safety. It's essential to value and explore our own intuitive abilities and not solely rely on external opinions or societal norms when assessing potential threats.

Self-reflection Questions

1. Are you trusting and listening to your intuition when it sends you signals about potential dangers or risks in your environment?

---

2. Have you considered that sometimes your expertise or judgment might hinder your ability to recognize valuable insights provided by your intuition?

_____

_____

_____

_____

3. Are you paying attention to seemingly unimportant details in your surroundings that could be essential signals your intuition is trying to convey?

_____

_____

_____

_____

_____

_____

_____

Life-changing Exercises

1. Trust your intuition in everyday decisions and reflect on how it influences your choices.

2. Practice noticing extra details in your environment, and try to understand their significance.

3. Challenge your expertise by embracing a beginner's mindset in new situations.

4. Keep a journal to record instances where your intuition guided you, and assess the outcomes.

5. Engage in mindfulness exercises to strengthen your awareness of your inner voice and gut feelings.

6. Identify situations where societal biases may be affecting your perception of risks, and consciously reevaluate them.

7. Share your experiences with intuition and survival signals with friends or loved ones to encourage open discussions and learning from each other.

Chapter 3: The Academy of Prediction

Key Lessons

1. The Importance of Introspection: Understanding human behavior and predicting violent tendencies in others requires introspection. By exploring our own feelings and experiences, we can better relate to and empathize with others, including those who may exhibit violent tendencies.

2. Recognizing Violence in Familiar Faces: Violent criminals often do not look like the stereotypical monsters portrayed in media. They may seem ordinary and even charming. Avoid the myth that violence comes out of nowhere and accept that perpetrators are part of the shared humanness of society.

3. Childhood Experiences and Violence: Childhood experiences, especially abuse and neglect, can significantly impact a person's potential for violent behavior later in life. Recognizing the importance of nurturing and providing a supportive environment for children is vital in preventing violence.

4. The Impact of Traumatic Events: Traumatic events, such as witnessing violence, can have lasting effects on individuals and influence their behavior and thought

patterns. Understanding the connection between personal experiences and behavior can aid in predicting violent tendencies.

5. Living in the Future: Some violent individuals, like the author himself during his troubled childhood, become adept at living in the future to avoid feeling pain or hopelessness in the present. This single-minded focus on the future can lead to recklessness and a lack of concern for personal safety.

6. Reactions to Shocking Situations: Violent individuals may display a lack of emotional response to shocking or distressing situations due to desensitization caused by their past experiences with violence. This emotional detachment can be a red flag when trying to predict violent behavior in others.

Self-reflection Questions

1. Have you ever considered how your childhood experiences might influence your thoughts and behavior as an adult, including your ability to understand others?

_____

_____

_____

_____

_____

_____

_____

2. Do you find it challenging to recognize potential danger in people who seem normal or even charming, and how can you improve your ability to see beyond appearances?

_____

_____

_____

_____

_____

_____

_____

3. When faced with shocking or distressing situations, do you notice any emotional detachment in yourself or others, and how can you better understand and address this response?

_____

_____

_____

_____

_____

_____

Life-changing Exercises

1. Childhood Reflection: Take time to reflect on your own childhood experiences and consider how they may have shaped your thoughts and actions as an adult.

2. Humanizing Others: Practice empathizing with people who might appear different or challenging to understand, recognizing their shared humanness and experiences.

3. Violence Awareness: Pay attention to news reports and analyze how violence is portrayed, looking beyond stereotypes to understand the complexities of human behavior.

4. Emotional Awareness: Develop mindfulness about your emotional responses in distressing situations, acknowledging any emotional detachment and seeking ways to connect with your feelings.

5. Personal Safety Assessment: Regularly assess your personal safety habits and mindset, identifying areas where you might be overlooking potential dangers or signs of violence.

Chapter 4: Survival Signals

Key Lessons

1. Trust your intuition: The chapter emphasizes the importance of listening to your intuition and recognizing survival signals. These signals are often subtle and can alert you to potential danger, helping you make informed decisions about your safety.

2. Beware of forced teaming: Be cautious when strangers use language that implies a false sense of shared purpose or experience, such as saying "we" or "both of us." This forced teaming tactic can be used to establish trust and manipulate victims.

3. Question excessive details: People with questionable motives often provide too many details in their interactions. Recognize this signal, as it can indicate deception or manipulation. Stay focused on the context of the interaction to avoid getting distracted by irrelevant information.

4. Be skeptical of unsolicited promises: Unsolicited promises are often used to convince you of someone's intentions, but they hold no guarantee. Treat promises with skepticism, especially if they are meant to persuade you to trust someone you are uncomfortable with.

5. Stand firm with the word "no": Never negotiate or give in when someone refuses to accept your boundaries and ignores the word "no." Trust and enforce your right to say no, especially in interactions with strangers, as it sets clear boundaries and avoids ceding control to potential manipulators.

6. Pay attention to body language and non-verbal cues: Non-verbal signals can speak louder than words. Both your own body language and the body language of others can provide crucial information about their intentions and character. Stay alert and attentive to these cues in your interactions with others, particularly in potentially risky situations.

Self-reflection Questions

1. Have you ever experienced a situation where someone used forced teaming language to gain your trust? How did you respond, and what could you do differently next time?

_____

_____

_____

_____

_____

_____

2. Reflect on a time when someone's charm and niceness made you question your initial instincts. How can you better distinguish genuine intentions from manipulative behavior in the future?

_____

_____

_____

_____

_____

_____

_____

3. Think about a situation where someone made unsolicited promises to you. How did you react, and how can you improve your ability to assess the sincerity of such promises moving forward?

_____

_____

_____

_____

_____

_____

Life-changing Exercises

1. Trust Your Gut: Practice listening to your intuition in everyday situations and make decisions based on your inner instincts.

2. Boundary Assertiveness: Role-play scenarios where you confidently say "no" to unwanted advances or offers, reinforcing your ability to set boundaries.

3. Critical Observation: Observe people's behavior and language for signs of forced teaming, too many details, or unsolicited promises, increasing your awareness of potential manipulations.

4. Mindful Interactions: During conversations, pay close attention to excessive charm or niceness and assess the speaker's true intentions before making decisions.

5. No Means No: Reinforce the importance of respecting your boundaries by standing firm and not negotiating when someone fails to accept your refusal.

Chapter 5: Imperfect Strangers

Key Lessons

1. The importance of understanding our intuition: Intuition is a valuable tool for predicting behavior and detecting potential threats. By paying attention to our gut feelings and subtle signals, we can assess the intentions and character of strangers more effectively.

2. Applying the "Rule of Opposites" in prediction: When making behavioral predictions, especially regarding safety, framing choices between contrasting options can help us arrive at more accurate conclusions. This technique frees us from the pressure of being right and allows intuition to guide our assessments.

3. Context matters in behavior prediction: People's behavior is influenced by the context they are in. To predict someone's actions, it's essential to consider the environment, circumstances, and their past behavior.

4. Identifying common ground with strangers: To better understand the behavior of strangers, it's helpful to find shared experiences or emotions. Recognizing similarities, even in vastly different situations, can provide insights into how they might perceive events.

5. Recognizing the significance of small cues: In the chapter, the author provides examples of seemingly minor behaviors or statements that can reveal important insights into a person's character. Paying attention to these details can aid in understanding potential threats.

6. Making predictions in advance: Effective prediction involves making assessments in advance, giving us time to prepare, take precautionary measures, or influence the outcome. Delaying predictions until the last moment may hinder our ability to respond appropriately to potential dangers.

Self-reflection Questions

1. Have you been paying enough attention to your intuition and gut feelings when assessing strangers' intentions?

_____

_____

_____

_____

_____

_____

2. When making predictions about someone's behavior, do you use the "Rule of Opposites" technique to explore contrasting options and arrive at more accurate conclusions?

_____

_____

_____

_____

_____

_____

_____

3. Have you been considering the context and past behavior of strangers to better understand their actions and potential risks?

_____

_____

_____

_____

_____

_____

Life-changing Exercises

1. Intuition Journal: Start recording your gut feelings and intuitions about people and situations. Review them regularly to develop a deeper understanding of your instincts.

2. Opposites Exercise: Practice framing choices between contrasting options to improve your ability to predict behavior and make more informed decisions.

3. Context Assessment: Before judging someone's actions, consider the circumstances and environment they are in. This exercise can lead to more empathetic and accurate evaluations.

4. Empathy Connection: Find common ground with others, even in vastly different situations, to enhance your understanding of their perspectives and feelings.

5. Predictive Planning: Cultivate the habit of making predictions in advance to allow yourself time to prepare, take precautions, or influence outcomes in various life situations.

Chapter 6: High-Stakes Predictions

Key Lessons

1. Predictions require understanding the language of behavior: Just like a dog expert can accurately predict a dog's behavior based on non-verbal cues, we can predict human behavior by understanding the signals and indicators that people exhibit. Non-verbal cues and gestures can convey important information about a person's intentions and emotions.

2. Intuition vs. Conscious Prediction: Intuition is the ability to listen to our instincts and make predictions based on gut feelings. It is often more accurate than conscious prediction, which relies on logical thinking. People, especially women, tend to be more intuitive and can make accurate predictions based on their instincts.

3. The importance of perspective: To make accurate predictions, we must try to see things from the perspective of the person whose behavior we are predicting. This means understanding their motivations, desires, and beliefs, even if they differ from our own. Seeing things from their point of view allows for a more accurate assessment of their likely actions.

4. Elements of Prediction (JACA): When making high-stakes predictions, it is crucial to consider four elements: perceived justification, perceived alternatives, perceived consequences, and perceived ability (JACA). Understanding these elements helps assess the likelihood of a person resorting to violence or other extreme actions to achieve their goals.

5. Context matters: The context of a situation is vital for making accurate predictions. Evaluating the surrounding circumstances, relationship dynamics, and environmental factors can provide crucial insights into the potential outcomes of a high-stakes situation.

6. Measuring Predictions: The success of a prediction depends on factors like measurability (how clear the outcome is), vantage (the observer's position to observe indicators), imminence (how soon the outcome may occur), context (clear understanding of the situation), pre-incident indicators (detectable cues before the outcome), and experience (knowledge and expertise on the topic). Considering these factors enhances the accuracy of high-stakes predictions.

Self-reflection Questions

1. Are you paying enough attention to non-verbal cues and gestures in others to better understand their behavior and intentions?

---

2. Have you considered the perspectives and motivations of others before making predictions about their actions or behavior?

_____

_____

_____

_____

3. When making high-stakes predictions, do you take into account factors like context, pre-incident indicators, and your experience to improve the accuracy of your predictions?

_____

_____

_____

_____

_____

Life-changing Exercises

1. Exercise intuition: Practice listening to your instincts in everyday situations and trust your gut feelings to guide decisions.

2. Perspective-taking: Regularly put yourself in other people's shoes to understand their viewpoints and motivations, promoting empathy and better relationships.

3. Non-verbal awareness: Pay attention to body language and gestures in conversations to enhance understanding and improve communication.

4. JACA evaluation: Apply the JACA elements (justification, alternatives, consequences, ability) when making important decisions to assess potential outcomes and risks.

5. Reflect on context: Before acting, consider the context and surrounding circumstances to make well-informed and thoughtful choices in high-stakes situations.

Chapter 7: Promises to Kill
(Understanding threats)

Key Lessons

1. Differentiating Threats from Intimidations: Understanding the distinction between threats and intimidations is crucial. Threats are statements of an intention to do harm with no conditions, while intimidations involve conditions to avert harm. Threats carry more likelihood of violence compared to intimidations.

2. The Power of Context: Context is more important than content when assessing the seriousness of a threat. Words spoken in specific situations or relationships can carry different meanings. Assessing the context helps determine the true intent behind the words.

3. Predictive Value of Threats: Threats are often used as a high-stakes manipulation to instill fear and anxiety in the victim. The threatener gains power through uncertainty, but once the threat is spoken, their actions are limited by the victim's response.

4. Gullibility towards Threats: People often overreact to threats, believing them to be more credible than they are. In reality, most threats are not acted upon,

and understanding the psychology behind threats can help reduce unwarranted fear.

5. Value Reduction Statements: Some threateners modify their initial threats or add alarming statements in succession. These value reduction statements often reveal a desire to vent anger rather than a genuine intention to cause harm.

6. Stay Calm and Perceptive: Reacting calmly to a threat allows for more mindful evaluation of the situation. Judgment can hinder accurate perception, so consciously asking if immediate danger is present helps to remain focused on the situation at hand.

Self-reflection Questions

1. How can you differentiate between threats and intimidations in order to assess the seriousness of a statement?

_____

_____

_____

_____

_____

_____

2. Have you considered the importance of context when interpreting the meaning behind someone's words?

_____

_____

_____

_____

_____

_____

_____

3. Are you prone to overreacting to threats and allowing fear to cloud your judgment, or can you stay calm and evaluate the situation objectively?

_____

_____

_____

_____

_____

_____

_____

Life-changing Exercises

1. Practice discerning threats from intimidations in your daily interactions to develop a clearer understanding of the underlying intentions.

2. Reflect on past situations where context played a significant role in shaping the meaning of words, helping you become more perceptive in future encounters.

3. Challenge yourself to respond calmly and rationally to alarming statements, resisting the urge to let fear control your reactions.

4. Engage in mindful evaluation of the credibility of threats, recognizing that most threats are unlikely to be acted upon.

5. Consciously avoid making value reduction statements when expressing anger, opting for healthier ways to communicate and manage emotions.

Chapter 8: Persistence, Persistence (Dealing with people who refuse to let go)

Key Lessons

1. Unwanted persistence can escalate into harassment: When dealing with individuals who refuse to let go, it is essential to recognize that their persistent behavior, when unwanted, can quickly escalate into harassment. Ignoring or failing to set clear boundaries with such individuals can fuel their pursuit.

2. Avoid engaging with unreasonable individuals: Trying to reason or negotiate with unreasonable people who refuse to let go often proves fruitless. Engaging with them may even exacerbate the situation, as they interpret any response as an invitation to continue their pursuit.

3. Limit the impact of harassment on your life: Victims of persistent individuals can regain control by limiting the impact of harassment on their lives. This may involve changing phone numbers, creating new email accounts, or employing other methods to insulate themselves from the harasser's attempts at contact.

4. Avoid making promises or commitments that aren't genuine: In dealing with persistent individuals, it is crucial to avoid making promises or commitments that aren't sincere or likely to be fulfilled. Such assurances may be misinterpreted and fuel the harasser's persistence.

5. Recognize the power of non-engagement: By not responding to harassment and not giving the harasser the attention they seek, victims can gradually diminish the harasser's motivation to continue their pursuit. Non-engagement communicates a clear message that their efforts are ineffective.

6. Seek help and support: Dealing with persistent individuals can be emotionally draining and stressful. Victims should not hesitate to seek help from friends, family, or professionals, such as law enforcement or experts in managing harassment cases, to devise a suitable management plan.

Self-reflection Questions

1. Have you recognized any signs of unwanted persistence in your life, and how has it affected your well-being?

---

2. Are you engaging with unreasonable individuals who refuse to let go, and if so, how can you limit the impact of their behavior on your life?

_____

_____

_____

_____

3. How can you practice non-engagement with persistent individuals to communicate that their attempts to contact you are ineffective?

_____

_____

_____

_____

_____

_____

Life-changing Exercises

1. Identify Unwanted Persistence: Take a moment to reflect on any persistent behaviors in your life that you find unwanted or uncomfortable.

2. Set Clear Boundaries: Establish clear and assertive boundaries with people who refuse to let go, and communicate them firmly.

3. Practice Non-Engagement: Refrain from responding to harassment or unwanted attention, allowing the persistence to lose its power over you.

4. Seek Support: Reach out to friends, family, or professionals if you encounter persistent individuals to develop effective strategies for managing the situation.

5. Reflect on Promises: Be mindful of the commitments you make, ensuring they are sincere and feasible to avoid unintentionally fueling persistence.

Chapter 9: Occupational Hazards (Violence in the workplace)

Key Lessons

1. Recognize Warning Signs: It's essential to pay attention to warning signs of potential violence in the workplace, such as verbal threats, aggressive behavior, or frequent expressions of anger. Ignoring these signals can be dangerous.

2. Trust Your Intuition: Intuition often provides valuable insights about potentially dangerous situations. If you feel uneasy or unsafe around a coworker, supervisor, or client, take these feelings seriously and assess the situation carefully.

3. Report Concerns: If you notice concerning behavior from a coworker or client, don't hesitate to report it to your supervisor, HR department, or security personnel. Promptly addressing these issues can help prevent escalation.

4. Establish Boundaries: Set clear boundaries with colleagues and clients to prevent potential abuse or harassment. Be assertive in communicating your comfort level and insist on respect for your personal space and boundaries.

5. Develop a Safety Plan: In high-risk situations or workplaces prone to violence, having a safety plan can be crucial. This plan may include knowing escape routes, having a reliable communication method, and understanding emergency protocols.

6. Understand Company Policies: Familiarize yourself with your organization's policies regarding workplace violence, threat assessment, and safety measures. Knowledge of these protocols will help you respond effectively if a threat arises.

Self-reflection Questions

1. Have you been paying attention to warning signs of potential violence in your workplace?

_____

_____

_____

_____

_____

_____

2. Are you trusting your intuition and taking it seriously if you feel uneasy or unsafe around someone at work?

_____

_____

_____

_____

_____

_____

_____

3. Do you know and understand your company's policies regarding workplace violence and safety, and are you prepared to act if a threat arises?

_____

_____

_____

_____

_____

_____

_____

Life-changing Exercises

1. Self-Awareness Check: Reflect on your reactions to coworkers or clients. Take note of any uneasy feelings or warning signs of potential violence.

2. Intuition Practice: Cultivate your intuition by regularly tuning into your gut feelings about people and situations in your life.

3. Boundary Setting: Practice asserting your boundaries with colleagues and clients to ensure respect and safety.

4. Emergency Preparedness: Create a safety plan for high-risk situations, outlining escape routes and communication methods.

5. Report and Communicate: Encourage open communication in your workplace about concerns and potential threats, ensuring prompt reporting to relevant authorities.

Chapter 10: Intimate Enemies (Domestic violence)

Key Lessons

1. Recognizing the Patterns of Abuse: Domestic violence often follows distinct patterns of control, manipulation, and abuse. Understanding these patterns can help victims and those around them recognize the signs of an abusive relationship.

2. The Power of Denial: Victims of domestic violence may be trapped in denial, minimizing or rationalizing the abusive behavior of their partner. It is crucial for friends, family, and support networks to be compassionate and patient while encouraging them to face the reality of their situation.

3. The Escalation of Violence: Domestic violence can escalate over time, becoming increasingly dangerous for the victim. Early intervention and seeking help can prevent further escalation and protect the victim from severe harm.

4. Breaking Free from the Cycle: Leaving an abusive relationship can be extremely challenging, and the period immediately after leaving is often the most dangerous. Having a safety plan in place and seeking

professional assistance can increase the likelihood of a successful escape from the abusive cycle.

5. Trusting Instincts and Seeking Help: Victims of domestic violence may sense danger intuitively but ignore or downplay these feelings. The chapter emphasizes the importance of listening to one's intuition and seeking help from professionals, law enforcement, or support groups.

6. Empowering Friends and Family: Friends and family members play a crucial role in supporting victims of domestic violence. Educating themselves about the dynamics of abuse and offering non-judgmental support can empower victims to seek help and break free from the cycle of violence.

Self-reflection Questions

1. Are you aware of the patterns of abuse in your relationship, and do you recognize any signs of control or manipulation from your partner?

_____

_____

_____

_____

_____

_____

2. Have you ever felt a sense of danger or unease in your relationship but dismissed or downplayed those feelings? How might you start trusting your instincts more?

_____

_____

_____

_____

_____

_____

_____

3. Do you know how to create a safety plan and seek professional help if you decide to leave an abusive relationship?

_____

_____

_____

_____

_____

_____

Life-changing Exercises

1. Pattern Recognition: Take time to identify patterns in your relationships and interactions. To encourage healthier connections, be aware of any indications of control or manipulation.

2. Intuition Tune-Up: Practice listening to your instincts. When you feel uneasy, pause and assess the situation. Trust your gut feelings and consider seeking advice or support if needed.

3. Escalation Awareness: Stay vigilant about any escalating aggression or violence in your relationships. Promptly address potential red flags and seek help from professionals or support networks.

4. Safety Preparedness: Develop a safety plan in case you find yourself in an abusive relationship. Know whom to contact and where to seek assistance if you need to leave.

5. Empowerment Support: Educate yourself and support friends or family who may be experiencing domestic violence. Offer non-judgmental support and encourage them to seek help and break free from the cycle of abuse.

Chapter 11: "I Was Trying to Let Him Down Easy" (Date-stalking)

Key Lessons

1. The Importance of Clear and Explicit Rejection: The chapter emphasizes the need for women to clearly and explicitly reject unwanted romantic advances. Being straightforward in stating one's lack of interest helps avoid confusion and sends a strong message to the pursuer.

2. Persistence Does Not Prove Love: The cultural notion that persistence in pursuit is a sign of love is debunked. In reality, persistent and unwanted pursuit indicates troubling behavior and a lack of respect for the person's boundaries.

3. The Power of No: "No" is a complete sentence and should be respected as such. Women are taught to be polite and accommodating, but it is crucial for them to assert their boundaries and firmly say "no" when they are not interested in pursuing a relationship.

4. Conditional Rejections Are Ineffective: Offering reasons or explanations for rejection often leads to further negotiation and confusion. Women are advised to reject unwanted advances unconditionally without giving room for debate.

5. Avoiding Negotiation: Continuing to engage with someone after an explicit rejection can be seen as negotiation and may fuel the unwanted pursuer's persistence. It is essential for women to avoid further contact or responses to such individuals.

6. Empowerment through Documentation: Victims of date-stalking are encouraged to document any unwanted communication or contact from the pursuer. Maintaining records of messages and encounters can be crucial for evidence if further action is needed to address the stalking behavior.

Self-reflection Questions

1. Are you clear and explicit when rejecting unwanted advances, using "no" as a complete sentence?

_____

_____

_____

_____

_____

_____

_____

2. Do you recognize that persistence from someone pursuing you does not necessarily indicate love but may be a sign of troubling behavior?

_____

_____

_____

_____

_____

_____

_____

3. Are you avoiding negotiation by firmly and unconditionally rejecting unwanted pursuits without giving reasons or explanations?

_____

_____

_____

_____

_____

_____

Life-changing Exercises

1. Practice assertiveness by clearly stating "no" without feeling the need to explain yourself.

2. Reflect on past experiences to identify any patterns of persistence in pursuing relationships and consider setting stronger boundaries.

3. Create a support network of friends or family who can encourage and remind you to stand firm in your rejections.

4. Document any instances of unwanted pursuit or stalking behavior to build a case for potential legal action if necessary.

5. Develop self-confidence and self-worth to recognize that you have the right to choose who is in your life, and you don't need to appease or accommodate others at the expense of your well-being.

Chapter 12: Fear of Children (Violent children)

Key Lessons

1. Early Warning Signs: Violent behavior in children often shows early warning signs. Parents and caregivers should pay attention to signs of chronic anger, cruelty to animals, fascination with violence, and an inability to control impulses. These warning signs may indicate a child's potential for violence and should not be ignored.

2. Media Influence: While media products like violent music and video games may not directly cause violent behavior in children, excessive exposure to graphic violence can desensitize them and influence their perceptions of violence as a means of recognition and significance.

3. Substance Abuse: The combination of substance abuse and violent tendencies in young people can lead to dangerous and aggressive behavior. Parents should be vigilant in addressing and seeking help for any substance abuse issues in their children.

4. Need for Intervention: Children who lack crucial emotional intelligence skills, such as empathy, self-regulation, and impulse control, are more likely to

engage in violent behavior. Early intervention, support, and guidance are essential to help these children develop these skills and prevent further violent tendencies.

5. Importance of Parental Responsibility: Parents play a crucial role in shaping a child's behavior and values. Neglecting the early warning signs or enabling violent behavior can exacerbate the problem. Taking responsibility for their child's actions and seeking appropriate help is essential for their well-being and the safety of others.

6. Recognizing Denial: Denial can be a dangerous factor in dealing with potentially violent children. Ignoring or minimizing warning signs can lead to tragic consequences. Acknowledging and confronting the problem, seeking professional help, and providing appropriate guidance and support can help address violent tendencies in children effectively.

Self-reflection Questions

1. Have you noticed any warning signs of chronic anger, fascination with violence, or impulse control issues in the children around you? How can you address these concerns proactively?

_____

_____

_____

_____

_____

_____

2. Are you aware of the media content and substance exposure of the children in your care? How can you ensure a balanced and healthy media consumption for them?

_____

_____

_____

_____

_____

_____

_____

3. Do you actively support and encourage emotional intelligence development in the children you interact with? How can you provide guidance and intervention to help them build empathy, self-regulation, and impulse control skills?

_____

_____

_____

_____

_____

_____

Life-changing Exercises

1. Reflect on Warning Signs: Take time to observe and reflect on any warning signs of violence or aggression in yourself or others. Awareness is the first step towards positive change.

2. Media Detox: Conduct a media detox by reducing exposure to violent content. Replace it with uplifting and educational media that promotes empathy and understanding.

3. Mindful Substance Use: If you consume substances, practice mindfulness to be aware of their effects on your behavior and emotions. Seek help if you find yourself struggling with substance abuse.

4. Emotional Intelligence Practice: Engage in activities that promote emotional intelligence, such as meditation, journaling, or attending workshops on empathy and self-regulation.

5. Take Responsibility: Recognize the impact of your actions on others and take responsibility for any harmful behavior. Seek guidance and support to develop healthier ways of expressing yourself and interacting with others.

Chapter 13: Better to Be Wanted by the Police Than Not to Be Wanted at All (Attacks against public figures)

Key Lessons

1. The Evolution of Idolatry: The media age has changed the nature of idolatry and adoration towards public figures. Previously, people admired public figures from afar, but with the advent of mass media, the behavior of fans has become more extreme and obsessive, leading to potentially dangerous situations.

2. The Dark Side of Fame: Fame can attract not only admiration but also dangerous obsessions from individuals seeking attention and notoriety. Public figures, especially those in the entertainment industry, may face the risk of being targeted by stalkers and attackers due to the increased exposure and adulation they receive.

3. The Pursuit of Attention: Some individuals with deep-seated emotional issues seek attention and publicity by harming or threatening public figures. Their desire for recognition and fame through violent acts can be fueled by media coverage and the notoriety gained from such actions.

4. The Fine Line between Admiration and Harm: It is crucial to distinguish between harmless admiration and harmful obsession. While most fans simply enjoy the work of public figures, a small percentage may develop dangerous fixations, and their behavior should be taken seriously and addressed appropriately.

5. Emotional Imbalance and Violence: Emotionally healthy individuals do not harm others. Public-figure attackers often suffer from emotional imbalances and personal issues that lead them to seek validation or revenge through violent acts against their idols.

6. The Role of Security: Attacks against public figures underscore the need for increased security measures, both personal and institutional. Proactive security measures can help prevent potential harm and protect public figures from dangerous individuals with harmful intentions.

Self-reflection Questions

1. Have you ever experienced extreme admiration or obsession towards a public figure, and how did you manage those feelings?

2. Do you recognize the potential risks and dangers associated with being a public figure, especially in the age of mass media and heightened idolatry?

3. Are you aware of your emotional balance and how it affects your interactions with others? How do you cope with negative emotions to ensure they don't lead to harmful actions or thoughts?

Life-changing Exercises

1. Reflect on your relationship with public figures: Examine your admiration and emotions towards public figures and identify any signs of extreme fixation or obsession.

2. Set healthy boundaries: Establish boundaries between admiration and unhealthy obsession with public figures, ensuring you maintain a balanced perspective.

3. Develop emotional awareness: Cultivate emotional intelligence to recognize and manage your emotions effectively, preventing them from leading to harmful thoughts or actions.

4. Practice empathy and understanding: Seek to understand the challenges and risks public figures face, and empathize with their need for privacy and security.

5. Increase personal security measures: Take proactive steps to enhance your personal security and safety, especially if you are a public figure or attract attention due to your profession or achievements.

Chapter 14: Extreme Hazards

Key Lessons

1. The Severity of Obsession: The chapter highlights the dangerous consequences of extreme obsession. Michael Perry's intense fixation on the public figure and his delusions led to a series of brutal murders. It emphasizes the importance of recognizing and addressing obsessions in individuals who may pose a threat.

2. The Power of Intuition: Intuition plays a significant role in predicting and preventing violence. Gavin de Becker's decision to relocate his client to a safe-house based on his intuition, even without concrete evidence, proved essential in protecting her from the danger posed by Michael Perry.

3. Assessing Risk Levels: The chapter demonstrates the critical process of assessing risk levels in potential threats. By categorizing Michael Perry as a high hazard individual, the author's team took appropriate measures to protect the client and actively pursued him to neutralize the threat.

4. Understanding the Mind of the Pursuer: By delving into Michael Perry's background and history, the book provides insight into the mind of a mentally ill pursuer.

This understanding is vital for authorities to develop effective strategies for apprehending such individuals.

5. The Impact of Childhood Trauma: The book explores how childhood trauma and abuse can shape an individual's psyche and lead to violent tendencies in adulthood. Michael Perry's troubled childhood and his mother's misuse of power played a significant role in his dangerous obsessions.

6. The Complexity of Stalking: The chapter sheds light on the complexity of stalking cases and how it can escalate into life-threatening situations. It emphasizes the need for proactive measures and thorough investigations to prevent harm to potential victims.

Self-reflection Questions

1. Have you ever experienced extreme obsession or fixation towards someone or something? How did you handle it, and did it impact your actions?

_____

_____

_____

_____

_____

_____

2. Can you recall a situation where you had a strong gut feeling about someone's intentions or behavior? Did you trust your intuition and take appropriate precautions?

_____

_____

_____

_____

_____

_____

_____

3. Reflect on the impact of your childhood experiences on your current behavior and attitudes. Are there any patterns that you recognize and may need to address for personal growth and self-improvement?

_____

_____

_____

_____

_____

_____

Life-changing Exercises

1. Self-Awareness Journaling: Reflect on your obsessions, thoughts, and emotions regularly to gain insights into your inner world and identify potential triggers for extreme behaviors.

2. Trust Your Gut: Practice listening to your intuition in various situations. Trust those instincts to guide you in making important decisions and staying safe.

3. Risk Assessment: Evaluate potential risks in your life and relationships. Identify any concerning patterns or behaviors in others and take appropriate precautions.

4. Childhood Healing: Explore any unresolved childhood trauma through therapy or self-reflection. Understand its impact on your current life and work towards healing and growth.

5. Boundaries and Safety Planning: Establish clear personal boundaries and develop safety plans for challenging situations. This ensures you are better equipped to handle extreme hazards effectively.

Chapter 15: The Gift of Fear

Key Lessons

1. Fear is a survival signal: Fear is not an emotion to be experienced constantly, but rather a valuable survival signal that alerts us to potential danger. It should be treated as a brief and informative message, guiding us to evaluate our environment and take appropriate action.

2. Trust intuition and evaluate fear signals: Honoring accurate intuitive signals without denial allows us to trust our instincts. By quickly evaluating the environment or situation, fear can dissipate, and we can respond effectively to real threats.

3. Unwarranted fear wastes energy: Continuously feeling fear of all people and situations diminishes its effectiveness as a survival signal. Learning to discern between genuine danger and imagined risks helps us direct our attention and focus on real threats.

4. Fear of specific outcomes: Fear is often linked to potential outcomes rather than the actual event. By understanding the links between fear and specific consequences, we can address our concerns more rationally and alleviate unnecessary anxiety.

5. Fear and worry are not the same: Fear occurs in the presence of danger and links to pain or death. Worry, on the other hand, is a self-imposed form of anxiety that often serves as a coping mechanism or avoidance strategy. Understanding the difference enables us to better control our emotions.

6. Embrace fear as a source of empowerment: Real fear can be an empowering force, providing us with the energy and focus to respond appropriately to dangerous situations. By acknowledging the presence of fear and using it as a guide, we can take decisive action when necessary.

Self-reflection Questions

1. How can you distinguish between genuine fear, which signals real danger, and unwarranted fear that wastes your energy and attention?

_____

_____

_____

_____

_____

_____

2. Have you ever linked fear to specific outcomes, and if so, how did understanding these links help you address your concerns more rationally?

_____

_____

_____

_____

_____

_____

_____

3. Reflect on a time when worry masked as fear affected your decision-making. How could acknowledging the difference between fear and worry have influenced your actions differently?

_____

_____

_____

_____

_____

_____

Life-changing Exercises

1. Daily Fear Evaluation: Take a moment each day to identify and evaluate any fears that arise. Ask yourself if the fear is based on genuine danger or if it is unwarranted worry. Practice redirecting your focus towards genuine concerns.

2. Fear Linkage Analysis: Identify a specific fear you have and explore the links it may have to other potential outcomes. Break down the fear into its underlying elements, understanding how it connects to various consequences, and assess their likelihood.

3. Intuitive Trust Building: Practice trusting your intuition by paying attention to subtle signals in your environment. Develop the habit of quickly evaluating situations and trusting your gut feelings. Gradually build confidence in your intuition's accuracy.

4. Fear Management Plan: Create a personalized fear management plan. List specific strategies for dealing with genuine fears and ways to redirect or dismiss unwarranted worries. Use this plan as a guide to navigate through different situations.

5. Fear-Focused Action: Identify a fear that has been holding you back from taking action in your life. Break it down into manageable steps, and take small, calculated actions to confront and overcome the fear.

Celebrate each success, no matter how small, and build momentum towards greater achievements.

Self-Assessment Questions

1. Chapter 1: "In the Presence of Danger"
- How does Gavin de Becker explain the role of fear in our lives when it comes to recognizing danger?
- What are some real-life examples from this chapter that illustrate the importance of listening to our instincts?

2. Chapter 2: "The Technology of Intuition"
- What does de Becker mean by "the technology of intuition" and how does it apply to our ability to sense danger?
- How can we sharpen our intuition and make better use of it in everyday situations?

3. Chapter 4: "Survival Signals"
- What are the key survival signals that de Becker identifies, and how do they manifest in potential threatening situations?
- Can you think of instances in your life where you may have ignored these signals, and what could you have done differently?

4. Chapter 5: "Imperfect Strangers"
- How does de Becker explain the concept of "forced teaming," and what are the potential dangers associated with it?

- What strategies does the author recommend for dealing with strangers who make us uncomfortable?

5. Chapter 7: "Promises to Kill" (Understanding threats)
- How does the author distinguish between "direct" and "indirect" threats, and why is this differentiation important?
- How can one determine the seriousness of a threat and take appropriate action?

6. Chapter 9: "Occupational Hazards" (Violence in the workplace)
- What are some warning signs of potential violence in the workplace, according to de Becker?
- How can employees and employers create a safer work environment and prevent violent incidents?

7. Chapter 10: "Intimate Enemies" (Domestic violence)
- What are the typical patterns and warning signs of domestic violence discussed in this chapter?
- How can we help someone who might be trapped in an abusive relationship?

8. Chapter 11: "I Was Trying to Let Him Down Easy" (Date-stalking)
- What are the indicators of "date-stalking" and how can we protect ourselves from this behavior?
- How can open communication and setting boundaries help prevent stalking situations?

9. Chapter 13: "Better to Be Wanted by the Police Than Not to Be Wanted at All" (Attacks against public figures)
- How are public figures often targeted, and what measures can they take to enhance their safety?
- How can the concepts discussed in this chapter apply to the safety of non-public figures as well?

10. Chapter 14: "Extreme Hazards"
- In this chapter, what examples does de Becker use to illustrate extreme hazards, and what lessons can we learn from them?
- How can we mentally prepare ourselves to respond effectively in life-threatening situations?

11. Chapter 15: "The Gift of Fear"
- According to the author, why is fear a gift, and how can we embrace it as a valuable tool in protecting ourselves?
- Reflect on a personal experience where your fear response was instrumental in keeping you safe.

12. General Reflection
- How has reading "The Gift of Fear" changed your perspective on personal safety and your ability to recognize potential threats?
- What practical steps can you take in your daily life to better utilize your intuition and safeguard yourself and others?

Made in United States
North Haven, CT
28 August 2024

56673300R00063